Fact Finders®

CAUSE AND EFFECT: The Bill of Rights

The Fourth Amendment:
Civil Liberties

BY JOHN MICKLOS, JR.

Consultant:
Richard Bell, PhD
Associate Professor of History
University of Maryland, College Park

CAPSTONE PRESS
a capstone imprint

Fact Finders Books are published by Capstone Press,
1710 Roe Crest Drive, North Mankato, Minnesota 56003
www.capstonepub.com

Library of Congress Cataloging-in-Publication Data
Names: Micklos, John, author.
Title: The Fourth Amendment : civil liberties / by John Micklos, Jr.
Description: North Mankato, Minnesota : Capstone Press, 2018. | Series: Fact
   finders. Cause and effect : The Bill of Rights | Includes bibliographical
   references and index.
Identifiers: LCCN 2017006678
ISBN 978-1-5157-7163-0 (library binding)
ISBN 978-1-5157-7176-0 (paperback)
ISBN 978-1-5157-7181-4 (eBook PDF)
Subjects: LCSH: Searches and seizures—United States—Juvenile literature. |
   United States. Constitution. 4th Amendment—Juvenile literature.
Classification: LCC KF9630 .M53 2018 | DDC 345.73/0522—dc23
LC record available at https://lccn.loc.gov/2017006678

Editorial Credits
Brenda Haugen, editor; Brent Slingsby, designer; Tracey Engel, media researcher;
Katy LaVigne, production specialist

Source Notes
Page 9, callout: Alfred H. Knight *The Life of the Law: The People and Cases That Have Shaped Our Society, From King Alfred to Rodney King*. Oxford, England: Oxford University Press, 1996, p. 123.
Page 10, callout: Thomas Fleming. "Defending the Family Castle, Part 1." *Chronicles: A Magazine of American Culture*, 24 March 2014. 25 April 2017. https://www.chroniclesmagazine.org/blogs/thomas-fleming/defending-the-family-castle-part-i/.
Page 13, callout: Linda R. Monk. *The Words We Live By: Your Annotated Guide to the Constitution*. New York: Hyperion, 2003, p. 158.
P17, callout: Ibid, p. 157.

Photo Credits
Alamy: REUTERS/Eduardo Munoz, 6; AP Photo: Yakima Herald-Republic, Gordon King, 5; Getty Images: Blend Images - Hill Street Studios, cover, Yellow Dog Productions, 28; iStockphoto: duncan1890, 9, KLH49, 15, traveler1116, 12; Newscom: George Frey/REUTERS, 27, JOHN GRESS/REUTERS, 19, JONATHAN ALCORN/REUTERS, 21, LUCAS JACKSON/REUTERS, 25, Olivier Douliery/ABACAUSA.com, 22–23, Rich Sugg/MCT, 24, TANNEN MAURY/EPA, 16; North Wind Picture Archives: 11, 13; Shutterstock: Dan Howell, 26, pixinoo, 29, Tischenko Irina, 7, cover design element; Wikipedia, public domain, 8

Design Elements: Shutterstock

Printed and bound in the USA.
010399F17

Table of Contents

Creating a
BILL OF RIGHTS

A loud knock on your front door disturbs your peaceful evening. You peek through your window. Two police officers stand outside.

"Let us in," one of them demands. "We got a tip there might be criminal activity going on here."

"You must have the wrong address," you reply. But the police officer knocks again. "You need to let us in," he says.

Do you need to let the officers enter? No. In most cases, the police need a **search warrant** to enter your home looking for evidence of a crime. Why? Because the Fourth **Amendment** to the U.S. **Constitution** protects people from unreasonable search and **seizure**.

The United States gained its freedom from Great Britain in 1783. Four years later, the nation's founders drafted the U.S. Constitution. This document described how the new government should be run.

The British had denied certain rights to the colonists. People worried that the new U.S. government might one day take away their freedoms as well. The authors of the Constitution addressed those fears. They added 10 amendments. They called these the Bill of Rights. Most of these amendments spelled out individual rights and freedoms.

FAST FACT:

The Bill of Rights started with 12 amendments. States failed to pass two of them, leaving just 10.

search warrant—an official piece of paper that gives permission to search a place for evidence
amendment—a change made to a law or legal document
Constitution—legal document that describes the basic form of the U.S. government and the rights of citizens
seizure—the act of taking something away from someone

The Fourth
AMENDMENT

Several amendments in the Bill of Rights listed protections people should have if charged with a crime. The Fourth Amendment gave guidelines for gathering evidence. Others cover the legal process, fair trials, and fair punishments.

The Fourth Amendment protects people against unreasonable search and seizure. What does this mean? Authorities can't search your house without a reason. The amendment also states that "no Warrants shall issue, but upon **probable cause**." Authorities must convince a judge to issue a search warrant. They must show that they will probably find evidence of illegal activity.

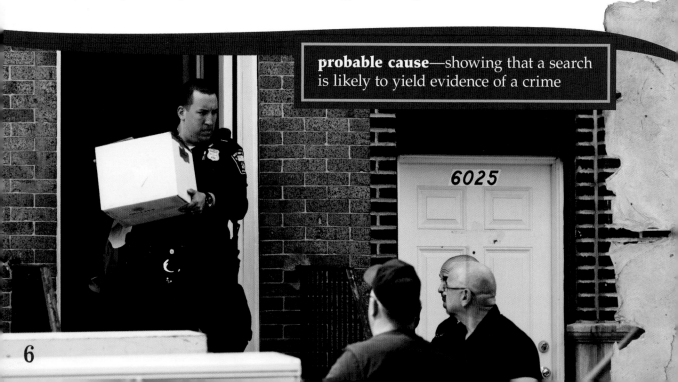

probable cause—showing that a search is likely to yield evidence of a crime

6025

The Bill of Rights

Amendment I

Congress shall make no law respecting an establishment of religion, or prohibiting the free exercise thereof; or abridging the freedom of speech, or of the press; or the right of the people peaceably to assemble, and to petition the government for a redress of grievances.

Amendment II

A well regulated militia, being necessary to the security of a free state, the right of the people to keep and bear arms, shall not be infringed.

Amendment III

No soldier shall, in time of peace be quartered in any house, without the consent of the owner, nor in time of war, but in a manner to be prescribed by law.

Amendment IV

The right of the people to be secure in their persons, houses, papers, and effects, against unreasonable searches and seizures, shall not be violated, and no warrants shall issue, but upon probable cause, supported by oath or affirmation, and particularly describing the place to be searched, and the persons or things to be seized.

Amendment V

No person shall be held to answer for a capital, or otherwise infamous crime, unless on a presentment or indictment of a grand jury, except in cases arising in the land or naval forces, or in the militia, when in actual service in time of war or public danger; nor shall any person be subject for the same offense to be twice put in jeopardy of life or limb; nor shall be compelled in any criminal case to be a witness against himself, nor be deprived of life, liberty, or property, without due process of law; nor shall private property be taken for public use, without just compensation.

Amendment VI

In all criminal prosecutions, the accused shall enjoy the right to a speedy and public trial, by an impartial jury of the state and district wherein the crime shall have been committed, which district shall have been previously ascertained by law, and to be informed of the nature and cause of the accusation; to be confronted with the witnesses against him; to have compulsory process for obtaining witnesses in his favor, and to have the assistance of counsel for his defense.

Amendment VII

In suits at common law, where the value in controversy shall exceed twenty dollars, the right of trial by jury shall be preserved, and no fact tried by a jury, shall be otherwise reexamined in any court of the United States, than according to the rules of the common law.

Amendment VIII

Excessive bail shall not be required, nor excessive fines imposed, nor cruel and unusual punishments inflicted.

Amendment IX

The enumeration in the Constitution, of certain rights, shall not be construed to deny or disparage others retained by the people.

Amendment X

The powers not delegated to the United States by the Constitution, nor prohibited by it to the states, are reserved to the states respectively, or to the people.

Causes of the FOURTH AMENDMENT

Cause #1: People wanted protection against abuse of warrants

In England, the government used "general warrants" to conduct searches. These warrants gave government officials great power. They could search anywhere at any time. They could seize anything they wanted. They entered people's homes or businesses without warning. They did not even have to explain what they were looking for.

In London in 1762, messengers sent by King George III broke into the home of John Entick. Entick had published articles criticizing the king. The messengers searched Entick's house. They broke locks and doors. They seized hundreds of papers. Entick sued the messengers for damaging his property. A judge ruled in Entick's favor. He said the messengers had no good reason for searching Entick's house.

John Entick

A year later British officials arrested John Wilkes and 48 other people. They accused the men of publishing insults toward the king. Officials searched the men's homes using a general warrant. Wilkes challenged his arrest. He called the search unfair. He won his case in an English court.

American colonists hoped British authorities would follow these rulings in the colonies. They did not. The British used general warrants to conduct searches of people's homes and offices. People lived in fear of such searches.

"Every invasion of private property, be it ever so minute, is a trespass."
—Lord Camden, British judge, 1765

Cause #2: People wanted to feel secure in their homes

No one wants to think about someone breaking into his or her home. The fear is even worse if the people breaking in are government officials. Shortly before the Revolutionary War (1775–1783), many colonists wanted independence from British rule. The British wanted to prevent this. They tried to silence leaders of the freedom movement.

Using general warrants, British troops made surprise raids. They burst into the homes of people they thought supported independence. Once inside, they searched the entire house. They seized personal items. They even read the person's letters. If these letters criticized the king or spoke out for independence, the person could be charged with **treason**.

"The poorest man may in his cottage, bid defiance to all the forces of the Crown."
—William Pitt, British leader, 1763

treason—betraying one's country

10

FAST FACT:

Colonists thought general warrants were unjust. After the Revolutionary War, states wrote their own constitutions. Eight of the 13 states banned general warrants.

11

Cause #3: People wanted their property to remain safe

The British placed a tax on sugar and molasses. Colonists thought the tax was unfair. To avoid paying the tax, they sometimes smuggled these goods into the colonies. The British often searched colonial ships and homes. They claimed to be looking for **smuggled** goods. But they sometimes seized other items as well.

Challenging Writs of Assistance

James Otis and 63 Boston merchants challenged the writ of assistance in 1761. Otis argued that these writs were unfair. He said the writs should state what areas would be searched and what officials thought they would find. Otis lost his case. However, the case brought more attention to the British abuse of colonists' rights.

smuggle—to bring something or someone into or out of a country illegally

customs agent—a government official who collects taxes and gives permission for ships to enter or leave a country

The British used writs of assistance to conduct these searches. This special type of general warrant gave British **customs agents** great power. Agents could enter any house or warehouse or board any ship. They didn't even need evidence that the place they planned to search actually contained smuggled goods. Agents often searched the ships and homes of innocent people. The colonists hated and feared these searches.

> "A man's house is his castle."
> —**James Otis, colonist, 1761**

Effects of the FOURTH AMENDMENT

Effect #1: Search warrants protected people from unreasonable searches

The Fourth Amendment gave peace of mind to citizens of the newly formed United States. Officials could not come into their homes for no reason. Most searches required warrants.

Law enforcement officers must get search warrants from judges. The Fourth Amendment states that these warrants must be issued with probable cause. Judges don't grant all requests for warrants. Judges must believe the searches will probably yield evidence of crimes.

Not all searches require warrants. For example, officers may see someone committing a crime. They can arrest and search the suspect. They also can search the area nearby for evidence. Officers do not need a warrant in emergencies. If they hear screaming inside a house, they can enter without a warrant.

The Fourth Amendment does not prohibit all searches. It only bans unreasonable searches. What makes a search unreasonable? The courts have wrestled with that question for more than 200 years.

SEARCH WARRANT

IN THE (STATE)_____COURT OF_____COUNTY,_____ACTION-LAW.

Number_____

Plaintiff/Petitioner:_____

vs

Defendant/Respondent:_____

QUALIFIED ORDER

Effect #2: People felt safe in their homes

Levels of Fourth Amendment protection depend on where people are. Courts have ruled that people can expect the most privacy in their homes. This goes back to the original reason for the Fourth Amendment. People didn't want law enforcement officers entering their homes without a reason. That is why police almost always need warrants to search people's houses.

People have less protection outside their homes. In one case, police inspected trash bags a person had put out by the curb. They found evidence of drug use. The Supreme Court ruled the search legal. The judges ruled that a person could not expect privacy once the trash was outside of his or her home.

> *"[The Fourth Amendment guarantees] the right to be let alone — the most comprehensive of rights and the right most valued by civilized men."*
> —**Louis Brandeis, lawyer and future member of the Supreme Court, 1890**

Legal or Illegal?

In one case, police thought a suspect was using high-intensity lamps to grow marijuana. They measured the heat coming from the suspect's house. They used this information to get a search warrant. Inside the suspect's house they found marijuana plants. The Supreme Court ruled that search illegal. On the other hand, courts have ruled that aerial **surveillance** of a person's backyard is legal.

surveillance—the act of keeping very close watch on someone, someplace, or something

Effect #3: People are protected if evidence is gathered illegally

What happens if police obtain evidence through an illegal search? According to the **exclusionary rule**, that evidence may not be used in a trial. For instance, police may have a warrant to search a suspect's home for weapons. If they also find illegal drugs, they may not use that evidence in court.

The exclusionary rule comes from two Supreme Court cases. The first case revolved around evidence seized from a house. There was no warrant for the search. The Supreme Court ruled that the evidence could not be used in court. At first the exclusionary rule only covered federal cases. A later case extended the rule to state cases.

Courts struggle to find balance in their rulings. They want to protect people's rights. At the same time, they do not want to prevent law enforcement officers from doing their jobs.

exclusionary rule—a rule saying that evidence gathered in an illegal search cannot be used in a trial
jurisdiction—legal power to interpret and administer the law in a specific area

Police search a home for drugs after securing a search warrant.

State vs. Federal Courts

The main difference between state and federal courts is **jurisdiction**. State courts handle a broad range of cases. These include traffic violations, family disputes, and most criminal cases. Federal courts only handle disputes involving the Constitution, laws passed by Congress, or cases involving more than one state. Sometimes a case might fall under both state and federal jurisdiction.

The Fourth Amendment
EVOLVES

For nearly 100 years, the Fourth Amendment drew little legal interest. The first major Supreme Court case involving this amendment did not occur until 1886. Customs agents seized some plate glass windows from John Boyd. They thought he was not paying the proper customs fees. The government forced Boyd to produce documents showing how much the windows were worth.

Boyd claimed it was unfair for the government to demand his private papers. He said it was the same as searching his office without permission. The Supreme Court agreed. It ruled that the Fourth Amendment covers more than just home searches. It also protects a person's private papers.

FAST FACT:

Students in schools have limited Fourth Amendment protection. A 1985 Supreme Court ruling upheld the search of a student's possessions at school. Random drug tests of students involved in sports or other activities also are legal.

The Fourth Amendment drew much more attention in the 20th century. New technology raised new questions. How did search-and-seizure rules apply to cars and airplanes? What about phones and the Internet? The courts had to decide. The courts also ruled on students' rights in school.

Police investigate threats made toward schools and students.

Fourth Amendment
TIMELINE

Some of the key Fourth Amendment developments and cases through the years include:

The nation's founders draft the Constitution. It outlines how the new government should work.

1787

1789 The founders draft the Bill of Rights. It spells out specific freedoms not listed in the Constitution.

The Bill of Rights is ratified and officially becomes part of the Constitution.

1791

1886 The case of *Boyd v. United States* says that being forced to turn over business records violates both a person's Fourth Amendment and Fifth Amendment rights.

In *Weeks v. United States*, the Supreme Court rules that illegally obtained evidence cannot be used in a criminal trial. This is called the exclusionary rule.

1914

1961 The *Mapp v. Ohio* case extends the exclusionary rule to states.

In *Terry v. Ohio*, the Supreme Court rules that police may frisk a suspect without a warrant if there is reasonable suspicion of illegal activity.

Police stand in front of the Supreme Court in 2012 after the Court ruled that police must get search warrants before using GPS devices to track criminals.

1968

1985

The Supreme Court rules in *New Jersey v. T.L.O.* that schools do not need probable cause to search students.

In *California v. Greenwood*, the Supreme Court says that police may search for drugs in garbage bags placed outside a house without a warrant. The court rules that the homeowner did not have a right to expect privacy outside of the house.

1988

The Supreme Court rules that a **sobriety checkpoint** set up in Michigan did not violate the Fourth Amendment rights of the people who were stopped and checked to see if they had been drinking.

1990

Congress passes the Patriot Act following the terrorist attacks on September 11. This act limits certain individual rights to protect public safety.

2001

2002

The Supreme Court rules in *Board of Education v. Earls* that a school district can require random drug tests for students participating in extracurricular activities.

The Supreme Court rules that placing a GPS device on a car to track it without a warrant is an unreasonable search.

2012

sobriety checkpoint—a place on the road where all cars are stopped to make sure drivers are sober

The Fourth Amendment
TODAY

Certain types of "blanket" searches do not require warrants. For instance, courts allow police to conduct sobriety checkpoints to catch drunk drivers. Such blanket searches are legal as long as they apply to everyone. Police can't **profile** people based on their age, race, religion, or gender.

Pretextual stops and stop-and-frisk checks also don't require warrants. In a pretextual stop, police stop a driver for a minor violation. Then they search for evidence of a larger crime. In stop and frisk, police briefly detain a person they think looks suspicious. They frisk the person in an effort to find weapons or drugs.

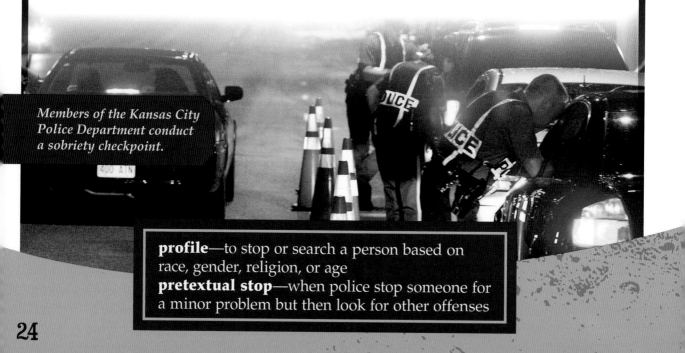

Members of the Kansas City Police Department conduct a sobriety checkpoint.

profile—to stop or search a person based on race, gender, religion, or age
pretextual stop—when police stop someone for a minor problem but then look for other offenses

Some people believe these types of checks help prevent crime. Other people think these checks violate people's rights. They point out that young African-American and Latino men are most likely to be searched. They believe police use profiling to make stops. In 2013 a federal judge ruled that New York City's stop-and-frisk program was unfair. It seemed to target minorities.

Stop and Frisk

A Cleveland, Ohio, police officer saw two men acting suspiciously. The men walked in front of a store many times. The officer thought they might be getting ready to rob it. He stopped the two men and a third man they had joined a couple of blocks from the store. He frisked them and found a gun on one of them. The man claimed the search was illegal. *In Terry v. Ohio* (1968), the Supreme Court upheld the arrest. The Court ruled that a brief search can be conducted if the police officer has reasonable suspicion of an illegal activity.

On September 11, 2001, terrorists struck the United States. Thousands died in attacks in New York City and Washington, D.C., and on an airplane that crashed in Pennsylvania. These attacks shook the nation. They also led to changes that affected people's Fourth Amendment rights. Soon after the attacks, Congress passed the Patriot Act. The act makes it easier for government officials to conduct searches. It allows them to search emails, voice mails, financial records, and medical records with only a basic search warrant.

Airport security also has grown tighter. In many airports, passengers must pass through full-body screening machines. They remain fully clothed, except for belts and shoes. The machines show if passengers are carrying anything dangerous. Some people object to the full-body scan. They say such screenings violate their right to privacy. Courts have ruled that full-body scans are legal.

the World Trade Center Towers after they were hit by airplanes

People realize that they have lost some privacy in this high-tech age. Websites track the pages they visit. Their cell phones track their calls and texts. Surveillance cameras watch busy traffic intersections. It is easier than ever before for the government to access this information if it wants to do so.

Many people are willing to trade some privacy for more safety. They believe they have nothing to hide. They don't care if the government is able to access some of their information. Others disagree. They believe that Fourth Amendment rights must be maintained. They fear the government may abuse the power to check up on people. They don't want to go back to the way it was under British rule.

A Transportation Security Administration (TSA) officer scans a woman in a full-body scan machine at an airport.

FAST FACT:

The Patriot Act allows law officers to use National Security Letters (NSLs) to gather evidence. The NSLs require banks, libraries, or other groups to turn over documents about a person. They do not require any warrant.

The amendments in the Bill of Rights have proven flexible. That's why they remain useful after more than 200 years. The words remain the same, but the way judges interpret those words has changed since the 1780s.

Rulings reflect changing needs and changing technologies. Over the last 100 years, the Fourth Amendment has been applied to cars, airplanes, phones, and the Internet. What other new technologies may emerge in the next 100 years? How might they affect the Fourth Amendment? Only time will tell.

The question remains: how do we balance personal rights with public safety? That discussion will shape the use of the Fourth Amendment in the 21st century.

Police can only search the trunk of a car if they have probable cause that a crime has been committed or if the driver allows it.

Security cameras are often used on streets and in businesses.

FAST FACT:

There were about 245 million video surveillance cameras in operation worldwide in 2014. The average American may be on camera as many as 75 times a day. They get filmed at stores, banks, traffic lights, and many other places.

A World Without Privacy

George Orwell's novel *1984* describes a society in which the government has complete power. Its slogan is "Big Brother is watching you." Cameras are everywhere. The government listens to everything people say. The secret Thought Police even try to find people who think thoughts against the government. People live in fear, even in their homes. Such a society goes against the Fourth Amendment.

GLOSSARY

amendment (uh-MEND-muhnt)—a change made to a law or a legal document

Constitution (kahn-stuh-TOO-shuhn)—legal document that describes the basic form of the U.S. government and the rights of citizens

customs agent (KUHS-tuhms AY-juhnt)—a government official who collects taxes and gives permission for ships to enter or leave a country

evidence (E-vuh-duhnts)—information, items, and facts that help prove something to be true or false

exclusionary rule (eks-KLOO-shuh-nahr-ee ROOL)—a rule saying that evidence gathered in an illegal search cannot be used in a trial

frisk (FRISK)—to feel a person's pockets and clothing in search of weapons or drugs

jurisdiction (joo-riss-DIK-shuhn)—legal power to interpret and administer the law in a specific area

pretextual stop (pree-TEKS-choo-ahl STOP)—when police stop someone for a minor problem but then look for other offenses

probable cause (PROB-uh-buhl KAWZ)—showing that a search is likely to yield evidence of a crime

profile (PROH-file)—to stop or search a person based on race, gender, religion, or age

search warrant (SURCH WOR-uhnt)—an official piece of paper that gives permission to search a place for evidence

seizure (SEE-zhur)—the act of taking something away from someone

smuggle (SMUHG-uhl)—to bring something or someone into or out of a country illegally

sobriety checkpoint (so-BRYE-uh-tee CHEK-poynt)—a place on the road where all cars are stopped to make sure drivers are sober

surveillance (suhr-VAY-luhnss)—the act of keeping very close watch on someone, someplace, or something

writ of assistance (RIT UHV uh-SIS-tuhnss)—a special warrant giving customs agents the power to conduct searches almost anywhere

READ MORE

Baxter, Roberta. *The Bill of Rights*. Documenting U.S. History. Chicago: Heinemann Library, 2013.

Krull, Kathleen. *A Kid's Guide to America's Bill of Rights*. New York: Harper, 2015.

Spier, Peter. *We the People: The Constitution of the United States*. New York: Doubleday Books for Young People, 2014.

Weinick, Suzanne. *Understanding Your Rights in the Information Age*. Personal Freedom & Civic Duty. New York: Rosen Pub., 2014.

INTERNET SITES

Use FactHound to find Internet sites related to this book.

Visit *www.facthound.com*

Just type in 9781515771630

Super-cool stuff! Check out projects, games and lots more at **www.capstonekids.com**

CRITICAL THINKING QUESTIONS

1. In what ways might people's lives be different today if there were no Fourth Amendment?

2. What experiences under British rule made citizens of the new United States feel strongly about the importance of the Fourth Amendment?

3. What information in the chapter titled "The Fourth Amendment Today" helps you see that there are different points of view about heightened use of searches?

INDEX